Explore Music through Poetry and Rhyme

David Wheway and Shelagh Thomson

17 varied national curriculum Music activities linked to the English attainment targets

Music Department
OXFORD UNIVERSITY PRESS
Oxford and New York

Oxford University Press, Walton Street, Oxford OX2 6DP, England

Oxford is a trade mark of Oxford University Press

First published 1993

Reprinted 1994

ISBN 0 19 321870 4

Design and illustration by Creative Intelligence, Bristol

Printed in Great Britain by Caligraving Ltd., Thetford, Norfolk

Acknowledgements

The Gobblegulp by Colin West © Colin West 1992

The Balloonist by Stanley Cook from *Another Third Poetry Book* ed. John Foster. Published by Oxford University Press © Stanley Cook

Noise by Jessica Pope © Basil Blackwell 1973, reproduced by permission of Simon and Schuster Education, Hemel Hempstead, UK

Fireworks by James Reeves. Printed with the permision of John Johnson (Author's Agent) Ltd., on behalf of the Estate of James Reeves.

Raindrops by Ted Harriot. We are unable to trace the copyright holder of this poem. We would appreciate any information which would help us to do so.

Contents

4 **Introduction**

List of Activities

8 Jack and Jill
9 Whispers
10 Trains
11 The Gobblegulp
12 Fishes
14 Peas and Honey
15 Masterpiece
16 Rhymes in Rounds
17 I Like the Sound of . . .
18 The Balloonists
20 Lyric Writer
21 Noise
22 Fireworks
24 Raindrops
26 Rap
28 Jabberwocky
30 Haiku

Appendix

31 Glossary
32 Pentatonic Scales

There are nine books in this series:

Explore Music through

Art, Geography, History, Maths, Movement, Poetry and Rhyme, Science, Stories, Word Games.

Introduction

These booklets are designed for primary teachers who value the role of music in an integrated approach to the curriculum. They are of equal value to those who have little or no experience of teaching music, or those who have responsibility as a music co-ordinator.

By closely relating musical activities to other areas of the curriculum, it is hoped that primary teachers will feel more confident when engaging in musical activities with children.

Within each of the nine booklets in the series, activities are ordered progressively from 'early years' through to upper Key Stage 2.

The appropriateness of any activity will depend on the previous experience of the child or group. For this reason we have not recommended any activity for a specific age group, but have indicated a target Key Stage.

Many activities, especially those primarily concerned with composition, are often best delivered over a number of sessions. This allows time for exploratory work, and also for evaluation, discussion, and development.

Building a Repertoire of Sounds

Children need an ever-increasing knowledge of sounds, and teachers need to be aware of the importance of sound exploration for future musical activities. This repertoire of sounds is especially important when children wish to represent feelings, objects, and other sounds in their compositions.

Body and Vocal Sounds

Children should explore the possibility for sounds made both vocally and with the body. For instance, how many sounds can be made with the throat? ('Ooooh', 'Ahhhh', a hiccup, a cough, a gargle, humming, sighing, panting, etc.) What different sounds can be made by patting different parts of the body? (Cheeks, chest, stomach, thighs, knees, etc.)

Classroom Percussion

Children should be encouraged to find as many different ways as possible to play percussion. Can it be scraped, tapped, shaken, scratched, blown, etc.? When a new sound is found, think about what moods or images it conjures up. Such exploration works well in small groups, using a limited number of instruments. Allow the children time to play new sounds to the rest of the class.

Percussion Resources

Some considerations when building resources:

Do your percussion resources offer a wide choice for creating a variety of sounds?

Are the instruments made from a variety of materials (e.g. wood, metal, plastic, etc.)?

Does the collection contain instruments from different ethnic origins?

Are the instruments of good quality? Remember, as in other areas of the curriculum, poor quality materials (e.g. worn or broken) may lead to poor or disappointing results.

Other Sound Makers

A wide variety of sounds can be made with everyday objects such as paper, kitchen utensils, beads and pulses (e.g. paper tearing, scrunching, flapping; pulses poured into a bucket, swirled around, shaken; pots and pans drum-kit).

When performing any activity, try different combinations of sound, as this adds to the children's exploratory work, and their understanding of timbre and texture.

Recording

It is very important that children develop ways of recording their compositions. A variety of ways are suggested throughout the booklets, for example, pictures, symbols, words, letters, and so on. Ensure paper and appropriate recording materials are always available.

Audio as well as video recorders are also valuable resources for recording children's work and development.

The Activities

Suggested Materials

These materials should be useful as a guide for preparing the lessons. They are only suggestions and teachers may wish to select their own materials.

Suggested Listening

Generally, it is a good idea to keep extracts short, e.g. 30–60 seconds in duration. If possible, tape-record extracts beforehand to avoid searching in the lesson.

Most of the suggestions given are easily available in record libraries or through record shops. Many can be found on compilations. Where this is not the case, a reference is given.

The recordings we have recommended should not be considered either obligatory or comprehensive.

Personal collections of recorded music are a valuable resource. However, do avoid limiting the children's listening opportunities to any one type of music.

Attainment Target Boxes

The left-hand box gives an indication of the main focus of each activity, relating to the national curriculum for Music. However it should be noted that the activities will also offer a variety of other musical experiences.

The right-hand box indicates how the activity may complement work undertaken in another area of the curriculum.

Classroom Organization

For many whole-class activities, a circle of children on a carpet or chairs is ideal. This helps concentration and promotes a feeling of involvement, as well as being practical when it comes to observing other children, whole-group involvement, and passing games. It might be advisable at times to split the class or set into groups.

There are some activities that require little or no percussion, and if you are just starting out you may feel more confident attempting these activities initially.

Handing Out Instruments

Avoid the children making a headlong rush to the music trolley at all costs! Allow the children to collect, or hand out, a few instruments at a time.

- Have the required instruments placed out ready beforehand.
- While listening to instructions, children should place their instruments on the floor in front of them.
- Give out beaters for instruments last.

- Before commencing agree on clear signals for stopping and putting instruments down (e.g. a hand in the air, a finger to the lips, a wink of the eye, etc.).
- Demand an immediate response to these signals.
- Encourage children to treat instruments with respect at all times. (This is not easy if instruments are worn or broken.)

Evaluation and Appraisal

When children are working on a composition, there should be regular evaluation by the teacher, and/or by the children, of how the work is progressing. This will include a great deal of purposeful listening and appraising. The process will in turn help the children in appraising the music of others.

Key Questions for Performers and Audience

Can you tell us about your music?

How did the piece start/finish?

What did you like about it?

What contrasts/changes did the piece contain?

Does the piece fulfil the task set?

Was it performed fluently and appropriately?

Could it have been improved, and if so, how?

Could the piece be extended, and if so, how? (e.g. repetition, contrasts, new material, different instruments, etc.)

Did the audience listen well?

The National Curriculum

The boxes at the foot of the page refer to the requirements for the National Curriculum for England, 1992. These have been superseded by the 1995 orders, but the areas of focus for both subjects are still relevant.

Jack and Jill

Suggested Materials

Access to a variety of percussion. Body and vocal sounds.

Rhyme

Jack and Jill went up the hill
To fetch a pail of water
Jack fell down and broke his crown
And Jill came tumbling after.

1. Sing the rhyme through together, tapping the pulse (beat) on knees.

2. Explore 'singing' the rhyme at a slower pace and a faster pace. Allow the children to 'feel' a common pulse on their knees each time before starting the rhyme.

3. Divide the rhyme up so half the children sing the first line, the others sing the second line, and then everybody sings the last two lines. Everybody continues to maintain the pulse on their knees/elbows/heads/noses, etc.

4. Explore singing the rhyme very quietly and then again louder, but not shouting.

5. Choose instruments to illustrate the various events in the rhyme, e.g.

Footsteps – claves, hands on table
Water – bell (water tap in the classroom?)
Jack falling down – cymbal, vocal cry
Jill tumbling – glissando on xylophone.

Can the children invent other sounds to go with the rhyme?

6. Say the rhyme, incorporating the sound effects.

Music Attainment Target: 1 & 2
Main Focus: Performing and Pulse
Key Stage: 1

English Attainment Target: 1
Main Focus: Traditional Rhyme

Whispers

Suggested Materials

Any rhythmic rhyme such as playground chants or nursery rhymes.

1. Once the children have learnt the rhyme, try performing in a normal voice and then whispering.
2. Now the children repeat the rhyme over and over, and on given signals from the teacher say the rhyme normally, or in a whisper. The teacher can change the way it is being said at any point in the rhyme. The signals from the teacher could be hands together (whisper), hands apart (normal voice).
3. Once the children are used to following the signals, repeat the activity, but instead of whispering they say the rhyme in their heads. Can the children still keep together? Find out by indicating a point at which they should begin speaking aloud and see if they are all at the same place.

Music Attainment Target: 1 & 2
Main Focus: Internal Pulse
Key Stage: 1

English Attainment Target: 1
Main Focus: Rhyme

Trains

Suggested Materials

Vocal and body sounds.

(NB See 'ostinato' in the glossary before proceeding.)

Down at the station, early in the morning,
See the little puffer trains all in a row.
Along comes the driver, pulls the little handle
Choo choo choo - and off we go.

1. Teach the children the above rhyme until they are all sure of the words.
2. Now teach the children an ostinato, using the first part of the fourth line – 'Choo choo choo (rest)'. The 'rest' is a silent beat. A group of children say this ostinato over and over, while the rest of the class say the rhyme all the way through.
3. The children might like to add some body percussion, e.g. rubbing hands as they say 'Choo choo choo (rest)'.

   Give all the children an opportunity to do the ostinato. (A song to try this idea with could be 'Three little ducks', using the 'Quack quack quack' as the ostinato.)

Music Attainment Target: 1
Main Focus: Rhythm
Key Stage: 1

English Attainment Target: 1
Main Focus: Rhyme

The Gobblegulp

The poem below offers the opportunity for a variety of sounds while it is being narrated. Incorporated into the poem are suggestions for sound, but obviously, encourage the children to invent their own sounds before relying on these suggestions.

The Gobblegulp by Colin West

The Gobblegulp is most uncouth	
In his mouth is just one tooth,	(single strike on Indian bells or high chime bar)
He gobbles food and gulps Ribena	(vocal munching, swallowing and slurping sounds, rattle of castanets)
Like a living vacuum cleaner.	(vocal humming, circular stroking on a tambour skins)
He has a great big bulging belly	(ascending notes on bass xylophone, blow up balloon)
That wobbles when he walks like jelly,	(flexi-tone if available, tambourines shaken)
But what I like about him least	
Is that he is a noisy beast,	(vocal 'Who . . . Me?')
For when he eats an apple crumble,	
His tummy starts to roll and rumble;	(wobble boards, roll on bass drum, vocal thunder sounds)
I often hear a noise and wonder,	
'Was that Gobblegulp – or thunder?'	(repeat some or all of the above sounds)

Music Attainment Target: 1
Main Focus: Exploring & Performing Sounds
Key Stage: 1/2

English Attainment Target: 1 & 2
Main Focus: Poetry

Fishes

Suggested Materials

Access to a variety of percussion. Vocal and body sounds.

One, two, three four, five,
Once I caught a fish alive.
Six, seven, eight nine, ten,
Then I let him go again.

1. The earlier activity '**Trains**', page 10, involved creating an ostinato from one line of a rhyme. However, with most rhymes it is possible to use two or even more of the lines to provide ostinatos. This idea can be tried with children who can already maintain one ostinato steadily.
2. Initially, have a small group of children saying the words, 'One, two, three four, five,' over and over. Notice how the words 'three four' are said in the same amount of time as each of the other numbers. Can the children now clap the rhythm of this line of the rhyme?
3. Once this is established, try with the ostinato group clapping their rhythm while the rest of the group say the full rhyme.
4. If the class can keep this going steadily, the children clapping the ostinato might like to try repeating their rhythm on percussion instruments.
5. Repeat the teaching of an ostinato to another group of children, this time using line two of the rhyme, 'Once I caught a fish alive'.

'One' 'Two' 'Three four' 'Five'

6. Once this is established, start the first ostinato group off – 'One, two, three four, five,' clapping or playing their rhythm on percussion. Then introduce the second ostinato group – 'Once I caught a fish alive,' so that both groups are playing together. It may take some practice before both groups can play together, and they will need to listen carefully to avoid getting faster or losing the rhythm.

   Once this is steady, the rest of the class say the whole rhyme over the ostinatos.

   Remember to let each group have a go at saying the rhyme and playing the ostinato parts.

7. Now try the rhyme at different speeds. Remember to indicate the speed before proceeding. (NB Slower is not necessarily easier.)

Extension Activities

Can the children find other rhymes to use, for a similar activity? Skipping rhymes and playground chants are useful sources.

Music Attainment Target: 1
Main Focus: Rhythm
Key Stage: 1/2

English Attainment Target: 1
Main Focus: Rhyme

Peas and Honey

Suggested Materials

Percussion including xylophones and other tuned instruments, arranged in a pentatonic scale (see Appendix).

Eat your peas with honey,
I've done it all my life.
It makes the peas taste funny,
But keeps them on the knife.

1. Teach the children the above rhyme then; following on from the previous activity, take the rhythm of the second and third lines. Practise playing them together, clapping initially and then using untuned percussion. These will later be used as an accompaniment.
2. Ask the children to clap the rhythm of the first line, 'Eat your peas with honey'. Then try playing this on tuned percussion using the pentatonic scale. Encourage children to keep their tunes simple, using notes that are quite close together, e.g.

   Eat your peas with ho - ney
   E D E D C C

   (It is important that the child can play this tune over and over rhythmically, in the same time as it would be said.)
3. When the children can maintain their melodies on tuned percussion, gradually accompany with the two ostinato parts, and play through while the rhyme is spoken.
4. Try adding a drone, using two of the notes of the pentatonic scale. Repeat these notes on the pulse.

Music Attainment Target: 1
Main Focus: Rhythm and Melody
Key Stage: 2

English Attainment Target: 1
Main Focus: Rhyme

Masterpiece

Suggested Materials

Enough percussion for the whole group, including tuned percussion with pentatonic scale (see Appendix).

This activity is intended to show how rhymes can be developed for use in ensemble work. The rhyme 'Eat your peas' (from **'Peas and Honey'**) is used as an example here, but most short, rhythmic rhymes can be used.

1. After spending some time inventing different tunes for the first line of the rhyme, the children should decide on three tunes that they will use. Give these tunes the names A, B, and C. (As the tunes are quite short, it might be useful if the letters represent each tune played through four times.)
2. Now decide on a sequence for these three tunes, e.g. Tune A – Tune B – Tune A – Tune C – Tune A.

   Repeating a tune, such as 'A' in the above sequence, can make a piece more interesting.
3. Once the order of the tunes has been established, use two lines from the rhyme as rhythmic ostinatos. These can be used as accompaniment. Begin both ostinato parts in turn. These play throughout. Once this is steady, incorporate into the tune sequence above.

Extension Activities

As a follow-up to this activity listen to pieces of music where a theme is often repeated e.g. 'Air' – from *The Water Music Suite* by Handel or 'Any Dream Will Do' from *Joseph and His Amazing Technicolour Dreamcoat* by Andrew Lloyd Webber. The chorus of a pop or folk song can also be a good example of a repeated theme. Count the number of times the theme is repeated.

Music Attainment Target: 1 & 2
Main Focus: Rhythm, Melody, and Form
Key Stage: 2

English Attainment Target: 1
Main Focus: Rhyme

Rhymes in Rounds

Suggested Materials

Access to a variety of percussion. Body and vocal sounds. A rhyme (most four-line regular rhymes will do), e.g.

Lots of little light bulbs
Shining all aglow
Bang go the fuses
Out they go.

1. Chant the rhyme together as a class, getting a feel for the rhythm.
2. Now attempt a round. Divide the class into two groups, A and B. Decide how many times through each group is to say the rhyme, e.g. four, and when they should start. Group A begins and when they have said the first two lines group B starts. Encourage the children to listen to each other and 'feel' the pulse together.
3. Once the rhythm is stable in both groups, try splitting the class into four groups, each group starting when the previous group has got to the end of the first line.
4. Try the above activity with the children clapping and saying the words.
5. Now try clapping only.
6. Finally, try playing the rhyme on percussion instruments.

Music Attainment Target: 1
Main Focus: Rhythm
Key Stage: 2

English Attainment Target: 1
Main Focus: Rhyme

I Like the Sound of . . .

Suggested Materials

Access to a variety of percussion. Large sheets of paper for group writing of poems.

1. Discuss favourite sounds with the children. Encourage them to share and listen to one another's ideas.
2. Ask the children, in groups, to write a poem such as the one below:

   I like the sound of . . . flip flops when I walk
   I like the sound of . . . sweet papers rustling
   I like the sound of . . . my pen against my teeth
   I like the sound of . . . birdsong, etc.

   (Lines don't have to rhyme, and line lengths can vary.)
3. Ask the groups to illustrate their poems using sound. What instruments can they find to illustrate the sounds in the best possible way? Can they incorporate these into a performance of the poem?

Extension Activities

The children could add another verse, e.g. 'I don't like the sound of . . . '

Music Attainment Target: 1 & 2
Main Focus: Composing
Key Stage: 2

English Attainment Target: 3
Main Focus: Collaborative Writing

The Balloonists

Suggested Materials

Access to a variety of percussion. Vocal sounds. Tape-recorder and recording of a current pop record or fairground music.

1. Hot-air balloons need constant blasts of hot air to keep them afloat. Ask the children to use vocal sounds to imitate the blast of the burner (e.g. blowing through closed teeth, lips slightly apart). This sound could be repeated over and over every ten seconds or so throughout the poem.
2. Add to this sounds that might represent floating, e.g. slow, steady pulse on chimes and Indian bells, occasional quiet pulse with soft beater on large cymbal, ascending and descending drone repeated on xylophone or metallophone.
3. Now use these sounds as an introduction to, and throughout, the poem. Other occasional sounds are suggested in the appropriate places.

Music Attainment Target: 1
Main Focus: Composing
Key Stage: 2

English Attainment Target: 1
Main Focus: Poetry

The Balloonists by Stanley Cook

Hot air rises	
And, their burners roaring	
As they pass overhead,	
The hot-air balloons	
Lift off from the fair.	(vocal cheers, bashing tins, taped pop music with volume control used to produce a decrescendo as the balloons rise in the sky)
Passengers upon the wind	
Arriving they don't know when	
They don't know where	
Below them	
Cars keep to the road	(distant, vocal hum of cars)
And trains to the track	(short back-and-forth scrape on tambour skin)
And high above them	
Jetting aeroplanes	(throat engine sounds, fading)
playing noughts and crosses	
With their vapour trails	
Return on radar	
To the runway.	
Holding on to their bubble of air,	
Balloonists alone	
Are free to follow	
Where the wind is blowing	
And the clouds are going.	(vocal wind sounds - then fade out all sounds)

Lyric Writer

Suggested Materials

A song that the children know well.

The children work individually or in small groups.

1. Choose a song that the children are very familiar with. It is easier if you choose one with short verses, e.g. 'Kumbayah', 'Twinkle, twinkle', 'What Shall We Do with the Drunken Sailor?', 'Frère Jacques', 'London's Burning', 'Hydom Hydom', 'Land of the Silver Birch', 'If You're Happy and You Know It'.
2. Write out the first verse of your chosen song, clearly and in lines. Look carefully at the structure. Count the syllables on each line, e.g.

Song	**Number of syllables**
Twinkle, twinkle, little star	7
How I wonder what you are	7
Up above the world so high	7
Like a diamond in the sky	7
Twinkle, twinkle, little star	7
How I wonder what you are	7

3. Ask the children to write their own verse, choosing their own subject matter. It may be useful to write one together as a class activity first.
4. Encourage the children to perform their verses to the rest of the class when finished.

A lot of useful discussion on syllables and scanning can result from this activity.

Music Attainment Target: 2
Main Focus: Matching Words to Rhythm
Key Stage: 2

English Attainment Target: 3
Main Focus: Writing Lyrics

Noise

Suggested Materials

Access to a variety of percussion.

Noise by Jessica Pope

I like noise
The whoop of a boy, the thud of a hoof,
The rattle of rain on a galvanised roof.
The hubbub of traffic, the roar of a train,
The throb of machinery numbing the brain.
The switching of wires on an overhead tram,
The rush of the wind, the door on the slam.
The boom of the thunder, the crash of the waves,
The din of the river that races and raves.
The crack of a rifle, the clank of a pail,
The strident tattoo of a swift slapping sail.
From any old sound that the silence destroys,
Arises a gamut of soul-stirring joys.
I like noise.

1. The poem refers to 15 noises. If you have a class of 30 children, they could work in pairs with responsibility for one sound.
2. Encourage very careful choosing of sounds. Initially the children might like to respond with vocal sounds, and then go on to finding these sounds and others on percussion. A procedure of selection and rejection should take place to arrive at the best possible sound.

Extension Activities

Try performing the piece with sound only. What cues do the children need to develop, to produce a fluent performance?

Music Attainment Target: 1 & 2
Main Focus: Composing
Key Stage: 2

English Attainment Target: 1 & 2
Main Focus: Poetry

Fireworks

Suggested Materials

Percussion and other sound makers, body and vocal sounds. Copies of poem (see next page). (If available, audio tape-recorder for recording and playing back.)

1. Read the poem to the children several times. Have copies for them to follow and read themselves.
2. Discuss the words and images involved. The task is to provide a 'backing track' (music/sounds) to accompany the narration of the poem.
3. The children could work in groups. Think about a general sound for the poem, that will continue throughout (e.g. crackling fire, 'Ooohs' and 'Ahhhs'). Think about sounds for:

   rising/falling, glowing/dimming, loud/quiet, spinning/slowing.

   Considerations:

   Are there any particular parts that could be highlighted? Are there any parts that could pose difficulties? Should the accompanying sounds start before the narration, at the same time, afterwards?

   Groups of children could work on one particular part of the poem.
4. Using a copy of the poem, the children could write down their ideas for sound, e.g.

	(one child shakes a tambourine quietly as the poem begins, and plays throughout)
They rise like sudden fiery flowers	(beaters run from bottom to top on glockenspiel)
That burst upon the night,	(cymbal crash)
Then fall to earth in bursting showers	(beaters from top to bottom on xylophone)
Of crimson, blue, and white.	(random notes on chime bars)

Fireworks by James Reeves

They rise like sudden fiery flowers
That burst upon the night,
Then fall to earth in burning showers
Of crimson, blue, and white.

Like buds too wonderful to name,
Each miracle unfolds,
And Catherine-wheels begin to flame
Like whirling marigolds.

Rockets and roman-candles make
An orchard of the sky,
When magic trees their petals shake
Upon each gazing eye.

Music Attainment Target: 1
Main Focus: Composing
Key Stage: 2

English Attainment Target: 1 & 2
Main Focus: Poetry

Raindrops

Suggested Materials

Access to a variety of percussion. Vocal sounds.

1. The poem on the opposite page can be used to develop a sound picture. Go through the poem carefully and discuss the images with the children. Some suggestions for sounds have been added.

   Practise and perform the poem in groups or as a whole-class piece, with a narrator.

Extension Activities

Try to perform as a piece of music without the narrator. This involves very careful listening by everybody. The children will have to decide how to space out the sounds. This might be done by using a short sequence created from the background chime bar music. The whole piece might be as follows: chime bar sequence x 2, *ladder music*, chime bar sequence x 2, *pathside pools*, chime bar sequence x 2 etc.

Experiment with different sequences and sounds. Discuss which performance the children prefer.

Music Attainment Target: 1
Main Focus: Composing
Key Stage: 2

English Attainment Target: 1 & 2
Main Focus: Poetry

Raindrops by Ted Harriot	(background sound of chime bars throughout)
On a rainy day I wish I	
Could climb	
A ladder of raindrops to the sky	(ascending notes on tuned percussion)
Could bathe	
In the glittering fresh pathside pools	(shaking bells)
Could leap	
Like a salmon up the gutter cascades	(guiro scraped, followed by triangle)
Could run	
In dribbles down the trunk of a tree	(slow glissando downwards on tuned percussion)
Could shake like a dog	
And see the spray fly from my hair	(shake tambourine)
Could bang and spatter	
Against the echoing tiles	(drum and claves)
Could gurgle	
Along the pipes above my room	(vocal sound)
Instead of that on days of rain	
I can only watch in indoor gloom	
The wrong side of the window pane.	(chime bars that have played throughout, slow down and fade)

Rap

Suggested Materials

Example of rap (see opposite).

Suggested Listening

Recordings of raps. These could be brought in by the children.

Raps are a form of rhyme that most children are very familiar with. Older children often prove surprisingly adept at producing short raps, which can be improved by adding a simple rhythmic accompaniment.

1. Before starting, discuss possible themes with the children (e.g. a visit to the dentist, common experiences at home/at school, factories, fashion, etc.).
2. Divide the children into small groups of about four or five. Initially, ask them to concentrate on a four-line rap.

   (Counting the number of syllables in their first line and trying to have the same number in the next three can help some children. In addition, if all children are writing about the same theme, their writings can be added together for a longer rap.)
3. As these initial attempts are quite short, they can be performed relatively quickly. Suggestions can be made by other children, and the performance can provide encouragement for any groups who are having difficulty. The feeling of success through performance can also act as encouragement for the groups to extend and improve their work. Children may like to try saying their rap to one of the rhythm accompaniments on an electronic keyboard. This is not as easy as the children might think, and needs careful listening and practice!

4. Once a rap is complete, ask the children to think of some sounds to accompany it. For instance, a visit to the dentist might go like this:

Went to the dentist the other day
Said all my teeth were on the decay
Showed me the drill, said, 'This won't hurt'
Ran for the door, but he grabbed my shirt.

One group says the rap, the other makes up mouth sounds with appropriate actions as an accompaniment throughout the rap, to the rhythm of the first line, e.g.

Went to the dentist the other day
sh sh sh sh sh sh rr rr ah

(sh = brushing teeth, rr = drill starting, ah = groan).

Music Attainment Target: 1 & 2
Main Focus: Composing and Rhythm
Key Stage: 2

English Attainment Target: 3
Main Focus: Collaborative Writing

Jabberwocky

Suggested Materials

See below.

The words of the poem 'Jabberwocky' are ideal for music-making, as they can be interpreted in any way the children wish.

1. The poem should be discussed with the class, and agreements reached, as to what the words might mean.
2. It might be a good idea to have some sounds that continue throughout the whole of the poem. These could be unusual electronic keyboard sounds, or eerie/sinister sounds on percussion. Vocal sounds recorded on a two-speed tape-recorder and then slowed down can be very effective. Other children can be responsible for sounds at certain points in the poem, and there are some suggestions below, although it is obviously better for the children to come up with their own ideas.

Jabberwocky by Lewis Carroll

'Twas brillig, and the slithy toves
Did gyre and gimble in the wabe:
All mimsy were the borogoves,
And the mome raths outgrabe.

(Guiro scraped repetitively, gently crumpled paper, monkey-type vocal sounds, fast alarm sound on triangle, crescendo roll on large cymbal, vocal hissing and buzzing.)

"Beware the Jabberwock, my son!
The jaws that bite, the claws that catch!
Beware the Jubjub bird, and shun
The frumious Bandersnatch!"

(Hissing vocal sounds, loud heartbeat on drum, all children rubbing legs/drumskins/tambour skins, woodblocks and claves for jaws, ripping paper, flapping paper for wings, vocal bird-of-prey sounds, straws sucking last drop of water in cup.)

He took his vorpal sword in hand: *Long time the manxome foe he sought –* *So rested he by the Tumtum tree,* *And stood awhile in thought.*	(Coconut shells for horses' hoofs, chime bars played to a slow, steady pulse plus melodic ostinato on xylophone, crumpled paper for leaves.).
And, as in uffish thought he stood, *The Jabberwock, with eyes of flame,* *Came whiffling through the tulgey wood,* *And burbled as it came!*	(Drums play steady pulse and crescendo, lots of paper sounds, cymbal crashes, vocal 'burbling' – an opportunity for a little humour here!)
One, two! One, two! And through and through *The vorpal blade went snicker-snack!* *He left it dead, and with its head,* *He went galumphing back.*	(Full scrapes on guiro, loud taps on claves, vocal 'snicker-snack!', coconuts/claves for horses' hoofs which get quicker.)
"And hast thou slain the Jabberwock? *Come to my arms, my beamish boy!* *O frabjous day! Callooh! Callay!"* *He chortled in his joy.*	(Followed by vocal cheering, which gradually fades. Repeat initial sounds as intro and accompaniment to last four lines.)
'Twas brillig, and the slithy toves *Did gyre and gimble in the wabe:* *All mimsy were the borogoves,* *And the mome raths outgrabe.*	

Music Attainment Target: 1 & 2 Main Focus: Composing Key Stage: 2	English Attainment Target: 1 & 2 Main Focus: Poetry

Haiku

Suggested Materials

Access to a variety of percussion. Haiku poems (see examples below).

1. Haiku is a Japanese form of poetry with three lines, which can be identified by the number of syllables on each line (5 - 7 - 5). It is a very expressive form of poetry and as such can encourage interesting mood music. It is also a form in which children can produce some interesting poetry.
2. The following are three examples:

Clouds sail slowly by
They grow heavy, full of rain
Thunder – the rain falls.

Silent deep river
Sudden rapids falling down
Churning wild water.

Football crowds jostle
'Goal!' Then roar dims to murmur
Homeward in triumph.

3. Divide the children into small groups, each responsible for creating mood music for a different haiku. Groups may like to think about choosing background sounds that can be played throughout to reflect the general mood (e.g. soft, low sounds for the 'deep river' haiku).

   They could add to this specific sounds to represent certain images, e.g.

   'rapids falling down' – a descending glissando on pitched percussion.
   'crowds jostle' – tambourines tapped or shaken.

Music Attainment Target: 1 & 2 Main Focus: Composing Key Stage: 2	English Attainment Target: 3 Main Focus: Writing Descriptive Poetry

Appendix

Glossary

Crescendo	Getting louder.
Decrescendo	Getting quieter.
Drone	One or more notes maintained throughout a piece.
Dynamics	The gradations of volume in music.
Form	The order in which different ideas appear in a piece of music.
Improvisation	Composing spontaneously while performing.
Glissando	The process of moving from one note to another quickly, while playing all other notes in between.
Notation	The symbolic written representation of sound(s).
Ostinato	A rhythm or melody pattern repeated regularly during a piece of music (often as accompaniment).
Pitch	The perception of sounds as 'high' or 'low' in relation to each other. A woman's voice is usually higher in pitch than a man's.
Pulse	A repetitive, regular beat (sometimes silent), which can indicate the speed of a piece of music.
Rest	'Musical silence' – the absence of a sounding note or notes.
Rhythm	The pattern which long and short sounds and rests make when heard in sequence.
Rhythmic independence	The ability to maintain a rhythm against other rhythms.
Score	A written record of all the parts in a piece of music.
Sequencing	The ordering of sounds.
Timbre	The characteristics/colour of sound(s).
Volume	The loudness or quietness of sound/music.

Symbols

f	Loud
p	Quiet
<	Getting louder
>	Getting quieter

Pentatonic Scales

The notes on tuned percussion should be arranged with long bars to the left, getting increasingly smaller to the right-hand side, and in alphabetical order. Most (but not all) start with 'C'.

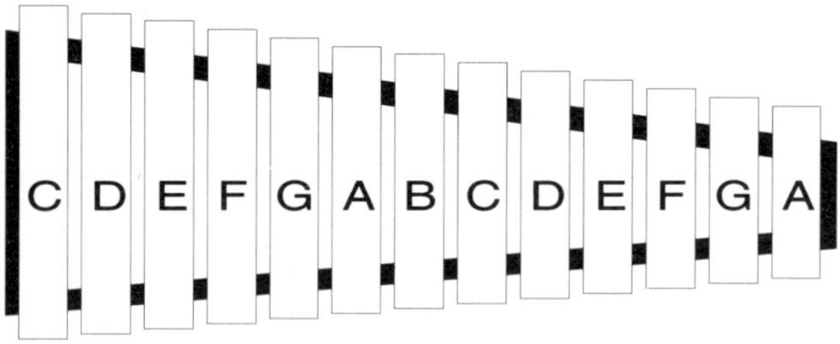

By removing any note 'B' and any note 'F', it is possible to have a five-note scale, called 'Pentatonic' (Penta = five). This should leave a sequence of C D E G A.

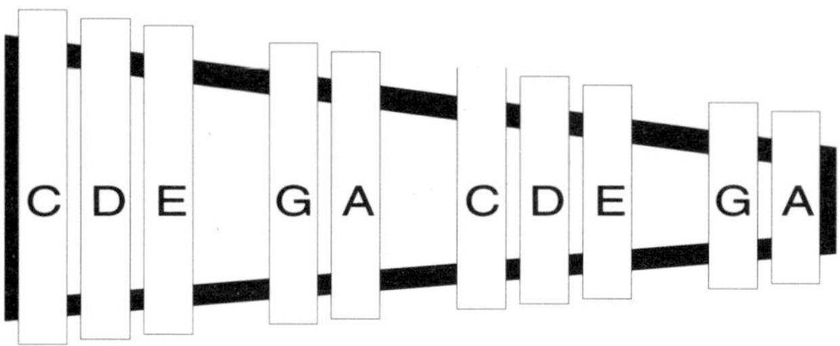

A pentatonic scale is useful for improvising melodies, both solo and in group work.

Occasionally instruments will come with notes called 'sharps' (with a ♯ after the letter), and 'flats' (with a ♭ after the letter), e.g. C♯ E♭ F♯ G♯ B♭. By using only these notes, it is again possible to create a pentatonic scale. This same scale can be found by just using the black notes on a piano or keyboard. Use this scale if most of the notes on your tuned percussion are sharps and flats.